The Journey

The Journey

Copyright © 2018 by Wendy Horger Alsup

First printing 2018

Printed in the United States of America

Unless otherwise noted, all Scripture quotations are taken from the Christian Standard Bible®, Copyright © 2017 by Holman Bible Publishers. Used by permission. Christian Standard Bible® and CSB® are federally registered trademarks of Holman Bible Publishers.

Scripture references marked NIV are from *The Holy Bible: New International Version*®, copyright © 1973, 1978, 1984 by International Bible Society. Used by permission of Zondervan Publishing House. All rights reserved.

The "NIV" and "New International Version" trademarks are registered in the United States Patent and Trademark Office by International Bible Society. Use of either trademark requires the permission of International Bible Society.

Scripture quotations marked NASB are from *The New American Standard Bible*®, copyright © The Lockman Foundation 1960, 1962, 1963, 1968, 1971, 1972, 1973, 1975, 1977, 1995. Used by permission.

Scripture quotations marked KJV are from the *King James Version* of the Bible.

All emphases in Scripture quotations have been added by the author.

All Hebrew definitions are from the Brown, Driver, Briggs, Gesenius Lexicon; which is keyed to the "Theological Word Book of the Old Testament" and accessed at www.biblestudytools.com. These files are public domain.

All Greek definitions are from a lexicon based on Thayer's and Smith's Bible Dictionary plus others; this is keyed to the large Kittel and the "Theological Dictionary of the New Testament," accessed at www.biblestudytools.com. These files are public domain.

Special thanks to my teen and my tween,
Luke and Ethan. I love you both dearly and
thank God I am on this journey with you.

Dear Parent,

I first wrote this journey through the Bible for my boys because I wanted them to learn the long story of Scripture that I did not personally learn until I was an adult. As a kid, I was taught Bible stories that seemed like disjointed moral lessons that at times contradicted each other. When I finally saw that all of the Bible from Genesis forward pointed to the coming of Jesus, the Scripture made sense to me in a way it never had before. I hope your son or daughter comes to understand the long story of Jesus in Scripture in youth in a way that equips them to serve God faithfully for a lifetime.

To help my boys with this study, I regularly asked them on the way to school or at the dinner table a simple question, "What did you read about today in your Bible lesson?" Then we talked about that day's straightforward reading and questions. I helped them make connections from story to story they may have missed, but I didn't pressure them or myself to make all of the connections in one sitting. This is a thirty week journey, and I found short, frequent conversations with my children more effective than long ones. I helped my boys notice repeated themes in Scripture, but our daily discussions were short unless they made a comment that caused me to stop and take more time with them.

Each weekly study starts with a short prayer encouraging readers to ask God to open their eyes to wonderful things in God's word. You might pray this with your children from time to time. Each week ends with a simple reflection on what readers learned about God and His plan for His children and how that lesson might apply to them today.

This is a simple study, yet one that I wish I had been able to go through myself in youth. I hope you notice the light come on in your children's eyes over time as they start to see the gospel threads winding through the various stories of God's children. May your family be blessed as your children grow in their understanding of the long story of Scripture that finds its fulfillment in Jesus Christ.

Wendy Alsup
mom to Luke and Ethan

Week 1

Pray: *Open my eyes, that I may behold wonderful things from Your law. Ps. 119:18 (NASB)*

Day 1

Read Deuteronomy 6:2-7. Why is loving God important? Why do you think we are starting our journey through Scripture with these verses?

_____

_____

_____

_____

_____

_____

Day 2

Read Matthew 22:34-40. Who is speaking? Where do you think He learned this truth?

_____

_____

_____

_____

_____

Day 3

Read I Corinthians 13:1-7. How would you describe Christian love to someone who had never heard the word before? How is the love that the Bible describes different from what we see sometimes in the world?

_____

_____

_____

_____

_____

_____

Day 4

Read I John 3: 7-11. What does loving others tell us about our relationship with God?

_____

_____

_____

_____

_____

_____

What did you learn?

Why do you think we started our journey through the Bible by reading about the Greatest Command? What did you learn about the things God desires for you? How does this matter in your life today?

_____

_____

_____

_____

_____

_____

_____

_____

_____

_____

_____

_____

_____

_____

_____

_____

_____

Week 2

Pray: ... *that the God of our Lord Jesus Christ, the glorious Father, would give (me) the Spirit of wisdom and revelation in the knowledge of him.* Eph. 1:17

Day 1

Read Genesis 1:24-31. To whom is God talking in verse 26?

_____

What does it mean that man was made in the image of God? Were animals made that way? What are some differences in humans who are made in God's image and animals that are not?

_____

_____

_____

Day 2

Read Genesis 2:15-25. What did God want Adam to do in the garden?

_____

_____

Why did God create woman?

_____

_____

_____

Day 3

Read Genesis 3:1-24. In verse 15, God says there will be enmity, hostility, or warfare between the woman and Satan. Woman's offspring will hit Satan in the head. Any idea who God might be warning Satan about?

_____

_____

_____

_____

Day 4

Read Genesis 6:11-22 and Genesis 7:11-24. Why was God angry with men on earth?

_____

_____

_____

_____

_____

_____

What did you learn?

What did the stories from this week show you about who God is?
What did you learn about God's plans for His children? How does this
matter in your life today?

_____

_____

_____

_____

_____

_____

_____

_____

_____

_____

_____

_____

_____

_____

_____

_____

_____

_____

Week 3

Day 1

Read Genesis 9:1-17. God used similar words with Noah that He used with Adam in Genesis 1:28-31. What did God tell Noah to do? Why do you think He repeated Himself?

_____

_____

_____

_____

_____

Day 2

Read Genesis 11:1-9. What was true of all mankind in verse 1? What happened to them at the end? Why do you think God did this?

_____

_____

_____

_____

_____

Day 3

Read Genesis 12:1-9. What did God ask Abram to do?

_____

_____

What does God promise to do for Abram?

_____

_____

_____

Day 4

Read Genesis 15:1-6. Why was Abram concerned that he didn't have any children? What did God promise him?

_____

_____

_____

_____

Why did God count or consider Abram righteous in verse 6?

_____

_____

_____

What did you learn?

What did the stories from this week show you about who God is?
What did you learn about God's plans for His children? How does this
matter in your life today?

_____

_____

_____

_____

_____

_____

_____

_____

_____

_____

_____

_____

_____

_____

_____

_____

_____

_____

_____

_____

Week 4

Day 1

Read Genesis 21:1-7. Why were Abram (now called Abraham) and Sarah surprised and happy when Isaac was born?

_____

What does verse 1 remind you about God?

_____

_____

_____

Day 2

Read Genesis 22:1-19. Why do you think God asked Abraham to sacrifice Isaac? Why do you think Abraham obeyed God?

_____

_____

_____

What did Abraham learn about God according to verse 14?

_____

_____

_____

Day 3

Read Genesis 25:19-34. Which son of Isaac and Rebekah's was born first? Which was born second?

_____

_____

What do you think a birthright is? Why did Esau give his to Jacob?

_____

_____

_____

Day 4

Read Genesis 28:10-22. Last week, we read about God's promises to Abraham in Genesis 12. Now God is speaking to Abraham's grandson, Jacob, many years later. What did God say to Jacob that He said years before to his grandfather, Abraham, as well?

_____

_____

_____

Why do you think God said these things again to Abraham's grandson?

_____

_____

_____

What did you learn?

What did the stories from this week show you about who God is? What did you learn about God's plans for His children? How does this matter in your life today?

_____

_____

_____

_____

_____

_____

_____

_____

_____

_____

_____

_____

_____

_____

_____

_____

_____

_____

_____

Week 5

Day 1

Read Genesis 37:1-36. How is Joseph related to Abraham?

_____

_____

Why did Joseph's brothers sell him into slavery?

_____

_____

_____

Day 2

Read Genesis 39:1-23. Why did Joseph do well in Potiphar's house according to verse 2?

_____

_____

Who took care of Joseph in prison according to verse 21? Why did He watch over Joseph?

_____

_____

_____

Day 3

Read Genesis 42:1-8 and 45:1-11. Why did Jacob send his other sons to Egypt?

_____

_____

_____

Why did God send Joseph to Egypt according to 45:5-7? What do you think would have happened to Abraham's grandson and great-grandchildren if Joseph hadn't gone before them to Egypt?

_____

_____

_____

Day 4

Read Genesis 50:15-26. How did Joseph respond to his brothers who had sinned horribly against him?

_____

_____

_____

Verse 24 is important. What does Joseph still believe God is going to do?

_____

_____

What did you learn?

What did the stories from this week show you about who God is?
What did you learn about God's plans for His children? How does this
matter in your life today?

_____

_____

_____

_____

_____

_____

_____

_____

_____

_____

_____

_____

_____

_____

_____

_____

_____

_____

Week 6

Day 1

Read Exodus 1:1-22. What happened to Abraham's great-grandchildren and their children's children in Egypt after Joseph died?

_____

_____

The job of the midwives was to help Israelite women when they had a baby. What did Pharaoh want the midwives to do? What did they do instead? Why?

_____

_____

_____

Day 2

Read Exodus 2:1-25. What did God hear in verses 24-25?

_____

Why did God help the children of Israel?

_____

_____

Day 3

Read Exodus 3:1-15. Why did God speak to Moses according to verses 7-8? Why was Moses afraid?

_____

_____

_____

What did God want Moses to tell the children of Israel in verse 15? Why do you think that was important?

_____

_____

_____

Day 4

Read Exodus 6:1-9. What did you learn about God in these verses?

_____

_____

_____

What did you learn about Moses and the children of Israel who had been slaves for a long time?

_____

_____

_____

What did you learn?

What did the stories from this week show you about who God is?
What did you learn about God's plans for His children? How does this
matter in your life today?

_____

_____

_____

_____

_____

_____

_____

_____

_____

_____

_____

_____

_____

_____

_____

_____

_____

Week 7

Day 1

Read Exodus 10:1-20. What reasons (more than one) kept Pharaoh from letting God's people go?

_____

_____

Why do you think God sent these plagues?

_____

_____

Day 2

Read Exodus 12:1-13. How were the Israelites supposed to protect themselves from the final plague against Egypt?

_____

_____

What kind of lamb were the Israelites to kill? Does this remind you of another story in Scripture? If so, how are the stories similar?

_____

_____

_____

Day 3

Read Exodus 12:33-42. What details do you notice when the children of Israel leave Egypt?

_____

_____

_____

Who was watching over them as they packed up and left?

_____

_____

_____

Day 4

Read Exodus 14:1-31. What do you notice about the children of Israel in verses 10-12? What did Moses tell them to do in verses 13-14?

_____

_____

_____

In verse 30-31, what was the result for God (see also verse 18) and the children of Israel?

_____

_____

_____

What did you learn?

What did the stories from this week show you about who God is? What did you learn about God's plans for His children? How does this matter in your life today?

_____

_____

_____

_____

_____

_____

_____

_____

_____

_____

_____

_____

_____

_____

_____

_____

_____

_____

Week 8

Day 1

Read Exodus 19:16-20:7. Now that the children of Israel are freed from Egypt, what is the first thing God wants them to do?

_____

_____

_____

Why do you think the first three commandments are about God and His name?

_____

_____

_____

Day 2

Read Exodus 20:8-17. What are these 7 commandments? Which are hardest for you to obey?

_____

_____

_____

_____

Day 3

Read Exodus 32:1-14. How are the Israelite's disobeying God? Why does this offend God so much?

_____

_____

_____

What do you notice as God and Moses talk in verses 11-14? Name at least three things.

_____

_____

_____

_____

Day 4

Read Numbers 13:17-33. Moses sent spies to look at the land God had promised to give them. What did the men see? Why were they afraid?

_____

_____

_____

Caleb spoke up with a different view. What did he believe?

_____

_____

_____

What did you learn?

What did the stories from this week show you about the things that are important to God? How does this matter in your life today?

_____

_____

_____

_____

_____

_____

_____

_____

_____

_____

_____

_____

_____

_____

_____

_____

_____

_____

Week 9

Pray: *Teach me, LORD, the meaning of your statutes* · · · . Ps. 119:33

Day 1

Read Leviticus 1:1-9. What kind of animals were the Israelites to bring to offer before the Lord?

_____

In verse 4, what do you think it meant for the animal to be accepted to make atonement for the person offering it? (hint: look at the definition of atonement in a dictionary.)

_____

_____

Day 2

Read Leviticus 16:1-16. The Holy Place in the Tabernacle held the Ark of the Covenant and the Ten Commandments. It symbolized God's presence with the Israelites. In verse 2, what would happen to Aaron if he came into God's presence without following God's instructions?

_____

What did God tell Aaron to do in verse 6 to atone for his sins? What do you think it means to atone for sins?

_____

_____

Day 3

Read Hebrews 6:19-20. Look back to Day 2. What was in the inner sanctuary behind the curtain?

_____

_____

Who has entered the inner sanctuary on our behalf? Hebrews calls Him a High Priest.

_____

_____

Who was the High Priest in Leviticus 16?

_____

Day 4

Read Numbers 21:4-9. Describe how the Israelites are speaking about God and Moses. Why did this offend God?

_____

_____

_____

What did God tell Moses to do to save the people? Does that remind you of another story in the Bible? How are they similar?

_____

_____

_____

_____

What did you learn?

What did the stories from this week show you about God's long plan to atone for the sins of His people? How does this matter in your life today?

_____

_____

_____

_____

_____

_____

_____

_____

_____

_____

_____

_____

_____

_____

_____

_____

_____

_____

Week 10

Pray: *Help me understand your instruction, and I will obey it and follow it with all my heart. Ps. 119:34*

Day 1

Read Numbers 14:1-25. In Numbers 13, ten spies gave a bad report about the land God was going to give to Israel. What is wrong with how the people respond in verses 1-4?

_____

_____

What is different about Joshua and Caleb's response in verses 5-9? Why do you think they have a different view?

_____

_____

_____

Day 2

Read Deut. 34:1-12. After wandering in the wilderness, the next generation was ready to finally enter the land God had promised to Abraham hundreds of years before. What happened to Moses? Describe him. What happened to Joshua? Describe him.

_____

_____

_____

_____

Day 3

Read Joshua 1:1-9. It's finally time! What is God going to do for which they have waited so long?

_____

_____

_____

What command did God say to Joshua several times? Why do you think Joshua needed to hear this again and again?

_____

_____

_____

_____

Day 4

Read Joshua 2:1-21. Name three things you notice about the woman who helped the spies. What does she believe about God? Why does she believe it?

_____

_____

_____

_____

_____

_____

What did you learn?

What did the stories from this week show you about who God is and what He loves? What did you learn about God's plans for His children? How does this matter in your life today?

_____

_____

_____

_____

_____

_____

_____

_____

_____

_____

_____

_____

_____

_____

_____

_____

_____

_____

_____

Week 11

Day 1

Read Joshua 6:1-25. Who fought the battle of Jericho? What did the children of Israel do? What did God do?

_____

_____

_____

_____

What happened to Rahab's family? Why?

_____

_____

Day 2

Read Joshua 24:14-31. After many years of fighting in the land, the children of Israel finally have their inheritance from God. What choice does Joshua want the children of Israel to make before he dies? What do they say they will do? Do you think they will do it?

_____

_____

_____

_____

Day 3

Read Judges 2:11-19. What happened in Israel after Joshua died? Why do you think this happened?

_____

_____

_____

_____

Who did God send to help Israel? What did they do?

_____

_____

Day 4

Read Judges 21:25. The book of Judges has many hard, sinful stories. It is a sad book. What are the two main problems during the time of Judges according to verse 25? Do you think people sin the same way today?

_____

_____

_____

_____

_____

_____

_____

What did you learn?

What did the stories from this week show you about who God is and what He loves? What did the stories show about our tendency toward sin? How does this matter in your life today?

_____

_____

_____

_____

_____

_____

_____

_____

_____

_____

_____

_____

_____

_____

_____

_____

_____

_____

Week 12

Pray: *Teach me good judgment and discernment, for I rely on your commands.* Ps. 119:66

Day 1

Read Ruth 1. Around the same time that every man did what was right in his own eyes in the book of Judges, what happened in Naomi's life? How did Naomi feel about all that had happened in her life?

_____

_____

_____

Day 2

Read Ruth 2. What does Boaz do for Ruth? Why does he do these things?

_____

_____

_____

Read Matthew 1:5, 6, and 16. Who was Boaz's mother? How are the stories of Rahab (in the book of Joshua) and Ruth connected to Jesus?

_____

_____

_____

Day 3

Read I Samuel 1. Why was Hannah upset?

_____

_____

What did she do? How did God answer?

_____

_____

_____

Day 4

Read I Samuel 3:1-21. Hannah's son, Samuel, now lives with the priest Eli. What happens to Samuel in this chapter?

_____

_____

_____

_____

In verses 19-20, what do you think it means that God didn't let any of Samuel's words fall to the ground?

_____

_____

_____

_____

What did you learn?

What did the stories from this week show you about who God is and His plans for His children? How does this matter in your life today?

_____

_____

_____

_____

_____

_____

_____

_____

_____

_____

_____

_____

_____

_____

_____

_____

_____

_____

Week 13

Day 1

Read I Samuel 8:1-9 and 9:15-21. What did the people want? How did God respond?

_____

_____

_____

How did God let Samuel know who should be king?

_____

_____

Day 2

Read I Samuel 15:1-23. How did Saul disobey God?

_____

_____

Read Deuteronomy 18:9-14. Though it's hard to understand why God commanded Saul to kill all of the enemy, what kind of things did some of them do that God did not want His children to do?

_____

_____

_____

Day 3

Read I Samuel 16:1-13. What do we learn about God in verse 7? How was God's view different than Samuel's view of who should be king?

_____

_____

_____

Why do you think God chose a different kind of king than Samuel thought He would?

_____

_____

_____

Day 4

Read I Samuel 17:12-50. Though the rest of the Israelite soldiers were scared of Goliath, David had a different response. Who did David believe was helping him? How did his faith in God help him?

_____

_____

_____

_____

_____

What did you learn?

What did the stories from this week show you about who God is and what is important to Him? What did you learn about God's plans for His children? How does this matter in your life today?

_____

_____

_____

_____

_____

_____

_____

_____

_____

_____

_____

_____

_____

_____

_____

_____

_____

_____

_____

_____

Week 14

Day 1

Read 2 Samuel 5:1-12. According to verse 2 and verse 12, why was David made king over Israel?

_____

_____

_____

Day 2

Read 2 Samuel 6:1-15. Why do you think all the people were excited that the ark of God was coming to the city of David?

_____

_____

Uzzah was killed, but the household of Obed-edom was blessed. Our God is to be feared, but He also blesses us for our good. What thoughts or questions do you have after reading this story?

_____

_____

_____

_____

_____

Day 3

Read 2 Samuel 7:1-17. What did David want to build for God?

_____

_____

What did God promise to do for David, David's son, and his descendants? How do you think God fulfilled that promised?

_____

_____

_____

_____

_____

Day 4

Read Psalm 103:1-22. This is a psalm written by David. What parts of his story do you think he is writing about? Name three things for which David praises God.

_____

_____

_____

_____

_____

_____

_____

What did you learn?

What did the stories from this week show you about who God is and what He loves? What did you learn about God's plans for His children? How does this matter in your life today?

_____

_____

_____

_____

_____

_____

_____

_____

_____

_____

_____

_____

_____

_____

_____

_____

_____

_____

_____

_____

Week 15

Pray: *Make your face shine on your servant, and teach me your statutes.* Ps. 119:135

Day 1

Read 2 Samuel 11:1-27. David broke three of the Ten Commandments. What were they?

_____

_____

_____

According to verse 27, how did God feel about what David had done?

_____

_____

Day 2

Read 2 Samuel 12:1-9. Who confronts David about his sin?

_____

To confess means to agree with God about your sin. David confessed his sin in Psalm 51:1-19. How did he agree with God about his sin?

_____

_____

_____

_____

_____

Day 3

Read I Kings 3:1-15. David's son Solomon is king now. What does he ask of God? How does God respond?

_____

_____

_____

_____

_____

Day 4

Read I Kings 6. What does Solomon build for the Lord? After hundreds of years of traveling around, the Ark of the Covenant finally had a permanent place to reside. What was in the Ark of the Covenant (see Deut. 10:5)? Describe how the inner sanctuary looked.

_____

_____

_____

_____

_____

_____

What did you learn?

This week, we read about David's sin, about Nathan confronting David, and about David confessing truthfully what he had done. When we confess a sin, it means we agree with God about what we did. God was faithful to forgive David, and He forgives us as well because Jesus died to pay for our sins. Is there anything you need to confess truthfully to God?

_____

_____

_____

_____

_____

_____

_____

_____

_____

_____

_____

_____

_____

_____

_____

_____

Week 16

Day 1

Read I Kings 11:1-13. What did Solomon do that displeased the Lord? What is going to be the result?

_____

_____

_____

Day 2

Read I Kings 12:16-24. King Rehoboam is Solomon's son. What happens to the kingdom while he is king? What tribes stayed with Rehoboam?

_____

_____

Here's a helpful summary from Bob Deffinbaugh at bible.org on the confusing history of Israel after this point:

> From this point on, the southern kingdom will be known as Judah, with Jerusalem as its capital and one of David's descendants as their king. The northern kingdom, composed of ten tribes, will be known as Israel. Samaria will eventually become its capital, and its dynasties will frequently change. At times, the two kingdoms will be at war with each other, and at other times they will make certain alliances. The glorious days of the united kingdom under Saul, David, and Solomon are gone. The northern kingdom will consistently have evil kings and behave wickedly. They will be the first to be scattered in judgment. The southern kingdom will have its good kings and its wicked ones, and eventually Judah will be taken into captivity by the Babylonians.[1]

---

1 https://bible.org/seriespage/21-great-divorce-kingdom-divided-1-kings-12-2-chronicles-10

Day 3

Read Jeremiah 1:1-19. What does God tell the prophet Jeremiah that He is going to allow to happen to the southern kingdom centered in Jerusalem?

_____

_____

According to verse 16, why is God angry with the southern kingdom? What commandments, that sit in the inner sanctuary of the temple right there in Jerusalem, have they broken?

_____

_____

_____

Day 4

Read Jeremiah 29:1-14. Though God's children are now living in exile in Babylon, God has not forgotten His promises to them. What does He tell them to do while they are in Babylon? What is God going to do for them?

_____

_____

_____

_____

_____

_____

_____

What did you learn?

What did the stories from this week show you about who God is and what is important to Him? What did you learn about God's plans for His children? Did God give up on His plans when His children sinned? How does this matter in your life today?

_____

_____

_____

_____

_____

_____

_____

_____

_____

_____

_____

_____

_____

_____

_____

_____

_____

Week 17

Day 1

Read Ezra 1:1-5 and 3:8-13. The temple that Solomon built had been destroyed. But what does God cause to happen that His promises will be fulfilled?

_____

_____

How did the young people feel about the new temple? How did the old people who remembered the first one feel?

_____

_____

_____

Day 2

Read Nehemiah 1:1-11. Not only had the temple been destroyed. What else was broken down at this time?

_____

How does Nehemiah describe God? What does he confess about the people's sin against God?

_____

_____

_____

Day 3

Read Nehemiah 8:1-12. After being exiled from the land because they turned away from God to worship idols, few Israelites knew God's words. How did they react when they heard the Scriptures read to them? Why do you think they reacted that way?

_____

_____

_____

_____

Day 4

Read Malachi 1:1-14. What problem did Israel still have? What was wrong with their sacrifices? What kind of sacrifice pleased God?

_____

_____

_____

_____

_____

_____

_____

What did you learn?

What did the stories from this week show you about who God is and what is important to Him? What did you learn about God's plans for His children? How does this matter in your life today?

_____

_____

_____

_____

_____

_____

_____

_____

_____

_____

_____

_____

_____

_____

_____

_____

_____

_____

_____

_____

_____

Week 18

Day 1

Read Malachi 4:1-6. What did God tell Israel to remember? What did God say He was sending?

_____

_____

Read Luke 1:5-24. Who did God send to fulfill His promise from Malachi 4?

_____

Day 2

Read Luke 2:1-40. In verse 4, why did Joseph go to Bethlehem instead of a different town? Why is this important (hint: see 2 Samuel 7:12-13).

_____

_____

Two old people at the temple recognized that Jesus was the fulfillment of the promises of God for which they had long waited. What are their names? What did they recognize in Jesus?

_____

_____

_____

Day 3

Read Matthew 1:1-25. What names do you recognize from stories we have read in the Bible up to this point?

_____

_____

_____

How does God refer to Joseph in verse 20? Why is this important?

_____

_____

_____

What does the name Immanuel mean?

_____

Day 4

Read John 1:1-8. What do you think it means that Jesus is the Word? What did the Word show us?

_____

_____

_____

_____

What was John the Baptist's role according to verses 6-8?

_____

_____

_____

What did you learn?

What does Jesus's birth show you about who God is and what He loves? What did you learn about God's plans for His children and how He keeps His promises? How does this matter in your life today?

_____

_____

_____

_____

_____

_____

_____

_____

_____

_____

_____

_____

_____

_____

_____

_____

_____

_____

_____

_____

Week 19

Day 1

Read Luke 3:1-20. What prophecy did John the Baptist fulfill?

_____

_____

What do you think John meant in verse 8 when he talked about bearing fruit that is consistent with repentance?

_____

_____

_____

Day 2

Read John 1:29-51. John the Baptist calls Jesus the Lamb of God who takes away the sin of the world. What is he referring to in the Old Testament?

_____

_____

In verse 45, what does Philip tell his friend about Jesus?

_____

_____

_____

_____

Day 3

Read Luke 4:1-15. Who tempted Jesus in the wilderness? Who helped Jesus through this temptation?

_____

_____

In verses 4, 8, and 12, what does Jesus use to combat Satan's attempts to get Jesus to sin?

_____

_____

What do you think it means in verse 14 that Jesus returned through the power of the Holy Spirit?

_____

_____

_____

Day 4

Read Luke 4:16-30. After Jesus read from the book of Isaiah, what did He mean when He said, "Today as you listen, this Scripture has been fulfilled"?

_____

_____

_____

Why do you think this made others in the synagogue angry?

_____

_____

_____

What did you learn?

What did the stories from this week show you about who Jesus is and what He came to do? What did you learn about God's promises to His children? How does this matter in your life today?

_____

_____

_____

_____

_____

_____

_____

_____

_____

_____

_____

_____

_____

_____

_____

_____

_____

_____

Week 20

Pray: *Help me understand the meaning of your precepts so that I can mediate on your wonders.* Ps. 119:27

Day 1

Read John 3:1-30. In verse 14, what is Jesus referring to from the past (hint: see Numbers 21:9)? What is He referring to in the future?

_____

_____

According to verses 16-18, who sent Jesus into the world? Why was He sent?

_____

_____

How does John the Baptist feel about this?

_____

_____

Day 2

Read Matthew 5. Many people are starting to follow Jesus. What does He teach in this chapter that stands out to you today?

_____

_____

_____

_____

_____

Day 3

Read Matthew 6. Jesus continued His long sermon to the people.
What important things did He teach in this chapter?

_____

_____

_____

_____

_____

_____

_____

_____

Day 4

Read Matthew 7. Jesus continued His sermon. What important things
did He teach in this chapter? What important thing do we see about
Jesus in the very last verse?

_____

_____

_____

_____

_____

_____

_____

What did you learn?

What did the Sermon on the Mount show you about who Jesus is and what He came to do? What did you learn from Jesus about God's plans for His children? How does this matter in your life today?

_____

_____

_____

_____

_____

_____

_____

_____

_____

_____

_____

_____

_____

_____

_____

_____

_____

_____

_____

Week 21

Day 1

Read Matthew 11. Why do you think John had doubts? Have you ever had doubts about Jesus? How did Jesus comfort John?

_____

_____

_____

What does Jesus teach us about following Him in verses 28-30?

_____

_____

_____

Day 2

Read Matthew 13:1-50. Jesus taught about the kingdom of God through parables (stories with hidden meanings) which He later explained to His disciples. What did you learn about the kingdom of God in this chapter?

_____

_____

_____

_____

_____

Day 3

Read Matthew 14:13-36. Right after John the Baptist was killed, Jesus went to a quiet place to be alone. What did the crowd do? How did Jesus respond? Why did He respond that way (see v. 14)?

_____

_____

_____

_____

What do you notice about Jesus and Peter's interaction in verses 28-33? Describe Peter's emotions. How did others in the boat respond?

_____

_____

_____

_____

Day 4

Read John 6:22-51. Why did people follow Jesus? Why does Jesus rebuke them?

_____

_____

The people wanted more regular bread to eat, but Jesus said He was the Bread of Life. What do you think He meant?

_____

_____

_____

What did you learn?

What did the stories from this week show you about God's plan for salvation compared to what the people wanted Him to do? What did you learn about Jesus and God's kingdom? How does this matter in your life today?

_____

_____

_____

_____

_____

_____

_____

_____

_____

_____

_____

_____

_____

_____

_____

_____

_____

_____

Week 22

Day 1

Read Matthew 21. This story begins the last week of Jesus's life. How did the people feel about Jesus at the beginning of this chapter? How did the Pharisees feel about Him at the end? Why do you think they disliked Him so much?

_____

_____

_____

_____

_____

Day 2

Read John 13:1-20. What did Jesus know was going to happen? How did Jesus feel about the believers whom God had given Him?

_____

_____

_____

What did Jesus want His disciples to learn by washing their feet?

_____

_____

_____

_____

Day 3

Read John 14:1-19. The disciples didn't understand that Jesus was about to die. How did Jesus prepare them? What did He teach them about where He was going?

_____

_____

_____

Who was God going to send to help the disciples after Jesus's death? What do you think it means that He would be their Helper (which can also mean Comforter or Counselor)?

_____

_____

_____

Day 4

Read John 17:1-26. Jesus prayed to God for the disciples He was going to leave behind. What important things did He ask God to do for them? See particularly verses 11, 15, 17, and 21. Did you notice that according to verse 20, He was praying for YOU too?!

_____

_____

_____

_____

_____

_____

_____

What did you learn?

What did you learn about God's plan from the things that Jesus did the last week before He was crucified? How does Jesus's prayer for YOU in John 17:20 help you in your life today?

_____

_____

_____

_____

_____

_____

_____

_____

_____

_____

_____

_____

_____

_____

_____

_____

_____

_____

_____

Week 23

Day 1

Read John 18:1-40. The Jews lived in their land, but they were under the rule of the Romans. What accusation did Jewish leaders bring to Pilate about Jesus? (see also Luke 23:1-2)

_____

_____

What did Jesus teach about His kingdom in verses 33-38?

_____

_____

_____

Day 2

Read John 19:1-42. Who most wanted Jesus to die?

_____

_____

Verse 30 teaches us something important. What do you think Jesus meant when He said, "It is finished"? What was finished or accomplished?

_____

_____

_____

_____

Day 3

Read John 20:1-31. What emotions do you think Mary, Peter, and the disciple Jesus loved (probably His brother James) felt before they discovered the empty tomb? What did they feel afterwards?

_____

_____

_____

To what individuals and groups did Jesus appear in this chapter?

_____

_____

Why did John write this book?

_____

_____

Day 4

Read Luke 24:13-35. In this passage, Jesus made a lot of things clear from the Old Testament to His disciples. According to verse 27, what did Jesus tell them?

_____

_____

What stories from the Old Testament do you think Jesus might have used to teach His disciples about Himself?

_____

_____

_____

What did you learn?

What does the story of Jesus's death and resurrection show you about God's plans for His children? What did you learn about the relationship between the Old Testament and the New Testament? How does this matter in your life today?

_____

_____

_____

_____

_____

_____

_____

_____

_____

_____

_____

_____

_____

_____

_____

_____

_____

_____

Week 24

Day 1

Read Matthew 28:1-20. What was Jesus's last instruction to His disciples before He returned to heaven?

_____

_____

In Genesis 1:28, God gave Adam a similar instruction. How is it similar to the Great Commission in Matthew 28? How is it different?

_____

_____

_____

_____

Day 2

Read Acts 1:1-11. Acts was written to Theophilus just like the book of Luke was. Some call it Luke Part 2. What happened in this passage (occurring right after the Great Commission we read about in Day 1)?

_____

_____

Who are the disciples waiting for? Why do they need Him?

_____

_____

Day 3

Read Acts 2:1-47. We continue to see the power of redemption through Jesus's sacrifice (redemption means to regain something that was lost through a payment of some kind). What story in Genesis did Acts 2 redeem (hint: see Genesis 11:1-9)? How was it redeemed?

_____

_____

_____

Many things happened after the disciples were filled with the Holy Spirit. Which ones stand out to you?

_____

_____

_____

Day 4

Read Acts 4:1-22. What do you notice about Peter in this passage compared to Peter at Jesus's crucifixion (hint: see Luke 22:54-62)? Why do you think he was different?

_____

_____

_____

What was happening among the people who heard about Jesus from Peter and John?

_____

_____

_____

What did you learn?

What did the stories from this week show you about God's plan for His people after Jesus returned to heaven? What did you learn about the Holy Spirit? How does this matter in your life today?

_____

_____

_____

_____

_____

_____

_____

_____

_____

_____

_____

_____

_____

_____

_____

_____

_____

_____

_____

_____

Week 25

Day 1

Read Acts 6:1-15. This passage describes the first deacons, those appointed to help with physical needs in the church so that pastors and elders could focus on teaching and spiritual oversight. Why did the church in Acts need deacons?

_____

_____

Read Acts 7:54-60. What happened to Stephen, one of the first deacons? Who else was there according to verse 58?

_____

_____

_____

(If you have time, read Stephen's sermon in Acts 7:1-53. It is a great summary of all we have studied in our journey through the Bible so far.)

Day 2

Read Acts 8:1-3 and 9:1-19. What interesting things stand out to you about Saul's conversion? This story is very important because Saul goes on to write at least thirteen books of the New Testament.

_____

_____

_____

Day 3

Read Acts 14:1-18. Who did the people mistake Paul and Barnabas for? What did Paul and Barnabas tell them in response?

_____

_____

_____

_____

_____

_____

Day 4

Read Acts 20:17-38. Where was Paul? Where was he going? What did he expect would happen to him when he departed?

_____

_____

_____

_____

_____

_____

What did you learn?

What did you learn about God's growing church, His children, from these stories? What testimony did Paul, Barnabas, and Stephen give to others? How does this matter in your life today?

_____

_____

_____

_____

_____

_____

_____

_____

_____

_____

_____

_____

_____

_____

_____

_____

_____

Week 26

Day 1

Read Acts 15:1-35. What issue arose in the church between Jewish believers (who tried to keep the Old Testament Law of Moses) and Gentile believers who were not originally a part of Israel?

_____

What did Peter teach in verses 8-11?

_____

_____

What did James teach in verses 19-21?

_____

_____

How did Gentile believers in Antioch react when they received the news of the council's decision by letter?

_____

Day 2

Read Read Galatians 1:1-12. Years later, the same issue from **Day 1** came up in the church at Galatia. How did Paul react?

_____

_____

Day 3

Read Galatians 2:1-21. We learned in Acts 15 that Gentile believers did not need to be circumcised and keep the Old Testament Law to be considered good Christians. What had Cephas (Peter) done in Galatia that Paul said was out of step with the gospel?

_____

_____

What important things did Paul teach about how we are saved in verses 15-21?

_____

_____

_____

Day 4

Read Galatians 3:1-29. How was Abraham saved according to verse 6? How did believers receive the Holy Spirit according to verses 2-5? How are we saved still today?

_____

_____

Paul teaches some complicated things about the Old Testament's (OT) relationship to the New Testament (NT). One easy thing to understand is that the NT doesn't say that the OT no longer matters. Instead, the NT **fulfills** the OT. In verses 19-26, what does Paul teach about the purpose of the OT Law?

_____

_____

_____

_____

What did you learn?

Are you a Jew or Gentile? What did the stories about this important early disagreement in the church teach you about how believers, Jew and Gentile, were saved then and are still saved now? How does this matter in your life today?

_____

_____

_____

_____

_____

_____

_____

_____

_____

_____

_____

_____

_____

_____

_____

_____

_____

_____

Week 27

Pray: *Make your face shine on your servant, and teach me your statutes.* Ps. 119:135

Day 1

Read I Corinthians 13:1-13. This week, we will read some of the Apostle Paul's important lessons to the early churches he founded. How would you describe love as the Bible uses the word to someone who had no idea what it meant? Why is love important in the church?

_____

_____

_____

_____

Day 2

Read Romans 8:1-39. What does verse 1 mean for you?

_____

_____

Are you experiencing hard things in life right now? What do verses 18-39 teach you about your suffering and the hard things that God has allowed in the lives of Christians over the years?

_____

_____

_____

_____

_____

Day 3

Read Philippians 2:1-18. In verses 1-8, what characteristic of Jesus does Paul want us to copy?

_____

Describe Jesus's humility.

_____

_____

Why do you think Paul warns against grumbling and complaining in verse 14? How do you think complaining might hurt you or others?

_____

_____

_____

Day 4

Read Philippians 3:1-21. Paul, who used to keep the OT Law very strictly, relied on something else to make him right before God. Describe how Paul relied on Christ and how that changed his life.

_____

_____

_____

_____

_____

_____

_____

What did you learn?

What are some of the important things Paul taught Christians at the churches in Corinth, Rome, and Philippi? How do these teachings matter in your life today? How can you apply them to things you are facing this week?

_____

_____

_____

_____

_____

_____

_____

_____

_____

_____

_____

_____

_____

_____

_____

_____

_____

_____

Week 28

Day 1

Read I Thessalonians 5:1-28. As believers waited on Jesus's return, Paul wanted them to respect the pastors or elders who were spiritual authorities in their lives. What other things did he want the people to do?

_____

_____

_____

_____

Day 2

Read 2 Corinthians 5:1-21. Our life on earth, which Paul likens to a tent, may be destroyed, but what do we have in heaven that we can count on forever?

_____

_____

What ministry has God given us according to verse 18? To reconcile means to restore friendships or to help enemies become family. How do you think God wants us to help others reconcile with Him and those they have hurt?

_____

_____

_____

Day 3

Read Galatians 5:13-26. We are free from obeying the OT Law, but instead of serving ourselves, how does Paul tell us to use our freedom in Christ?

_____

_____

What do you think it means to walk with the Holy Spirit? What kinds of things will we see in our lives when we walk with the Spirit?

_____

_____

_____

_____

Day 4

Read Titus 1:4-9. What kind of men did Paul want Titus to appoint to be spiritual leaders in the church? What was the elder supposed to do in the church according to verse 9?

_____

_____

_____

Read I Timothy 3:1-13. Paul described the qualities of good elders and good deacons. How should we view faithful elders and deacons in our churches according to verses 1 and 13?

_____

_____

_____

_____

What did you learn?

This week, we read about aspects of life in the early church which still matter in our churches today. What lessons seem to matter most for your life and your church right now?

_____

_____

_____

_____

_____

_____

_____

_____

_____

_____

_____

_____

_____

_____

_____

_____

_____

_____

_____

Week 29

Day 1

Read Hebrews 9:1-28. As we enter the last weeks of our journey through Scripture, the author of Hebrews wants to make sure we understand how Jesus fulfilled the OT Law and saved us once for all from our sin. With help from verses 11-14, describe the link between the OT tabernacle and sacrifices and Christ's sacrifice on the cross.

_____

_____

_____

_____

_____

Day 2

Read Hebrews 10:1-25. According to verses 1-4, what was the problem with sacrifices in the OT?

_____

_____

What do verses 19-25 teach about the result of Christ's sacrifice for us? What can and should we confidently do now?

_____

_____

_____

Day 3

Read Hebrews 11:1-40. How would you describe faith to someone who doesn't know what the word means (hint: see verses 1 and 6)?

_____

_____

What do verses 13-16 teach you about the faith of the people this chapter mentions?

_____

_____

_____

_____

Day 4

Read Hebrews 12:1-17. The author wrote to encourage those who were persecuted for their faith and enduring a long trial. What encourages us to endure hard things according to verses 1-3?

_____

_____

_____

In verses 7-11, we are taught that God's discipline (training in righteousness) can be hard. How is it also good for us?

_____

_____

_____

_____

What did you learn?

What did the Bible reading from this week remind you about who God is and what He has done for you? Are you facing a hard thing in your life right now? How do these verses in the Bible help you?

_____

_____

_____

_____

_____

_____

_____

_____

_____

_____

_____

_____

_____

_____

_____

_____

_____

_____

Week 30

Day 1

Read Revelation 1:1-20. Christians disagree about some of the details of how the end times play out. But some things are clear. According to verses 1 and 4-8, who is revealed in Revelation?

_____

What do you think it means that Jesus Christ is the Alpha and Omega (the first and last letters of the Greek alphabet)? (Hint: see verse 17)

_____

_____

_____

_____

Day 2

Read Revelation 4:1-11. Who is the focal point of this passage? What kind of things are men and creatures saying about Him?

_____

_____

Read Revelations 5:6-14. Who is being praised? Why are they praising Him? What do they say about Him?

_____

_____

_____

Day 3

Read Revelation 19:6-10. Who is the lamb? Who is His bride? (hint: see Ephesians 5:25-27)

_____

_____

How does Ephesians 5:25-27 help you understand Revelation 19:8? What do you think both are teaching?

_____

_____

_____

_____

_____

Day 4

Read Revelation 21:1-8 and Revelation 22:20-21. Though some Christians disagree about how the end times play out, we all know for sure that it ends with Jesus's return and happy eternal life for all believers. How does Revelation describe the joyful things those of us who believe in Jesus Christ will experience in eternity?

_____

_____

_____

_____

_____

_____

What did you learn?

As we end our journey through Scripture, what did you learn overall about the relationship between the Old Testament and the New Testament? What did you learn about Jesus in the Old Testament? What did you learn this week from Revelation about our hope for the future? How does this matter in your life today?

_____

_____

_____

_____

_____

_____

_____

_____

_____

_____

_____

_____

_____

_____

_____

_____

_____

_____

_____

_____

Manufactured by Amazon.ca
Bolton, ON